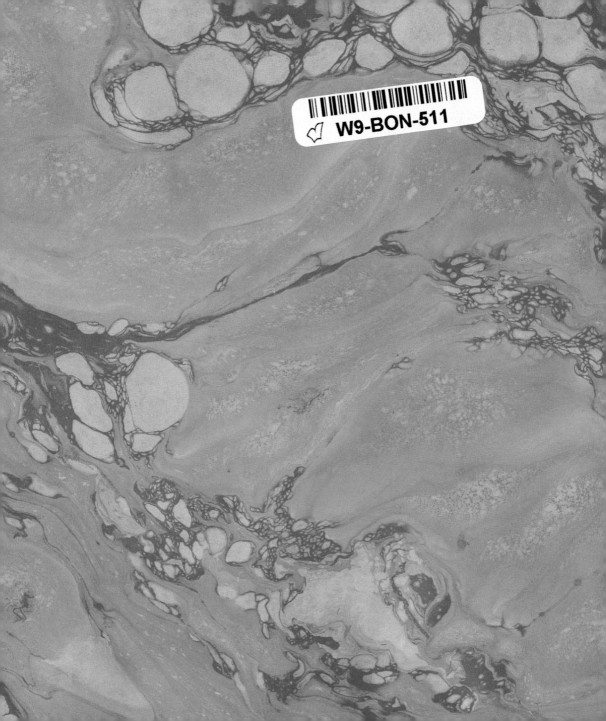

a wine lover's journal

whitecap

© Copyright 1998 by Whitecap Books
Introductory text written by Clare Rundall, in consultation with John Moore.

Fourth Printing, 2003

Printed and bound in Canada by Friesens, Altona, Manitoba.

National Library of Canada Cataloguing in Publication Data
Rundall, Clare.
A wine lover's journal

ISBN 1-55285-454-X

1. Wine and wine making—Miscellanea. 2. Wine tasting—
Miscellanea. I. Moore, John. II. Title.
TP548.R86 2003   641.2'2   C2003-910238-6

The publisher acknowledges the support of the Canada Council for the Arts and
the Cultural Services Branch of the Government of British Columbia for our
publishing program. We acknowledge the financial support of the Government
of Canada through the Book Industry Development Program for our publishing
activities.

Table of Contents

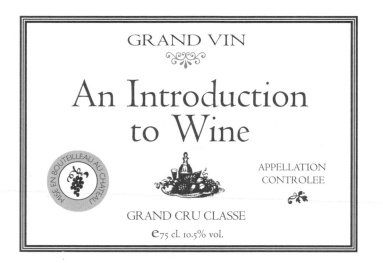

GRAND VIN

An Introduction to Wine

APPELLATION
CONTROLEE

GRAND CRU CLASSE

e 75 cl. 10.5% vol.

Visiting a Winery

A visit to a winery is excellent encouragement to start collecting wine.
Tours often include a sampling of raw and aged wine. It is wise to call
ahead before visiting, as many wineries are family-run or small businesses.
April, May and September are good months to visit vineyards. Refer to
"The North American Vintner's Year" as a guide to the vineyard's schedule.

Vineyards can be muddy and cellars can be cool, so dress appropriately.
It's impolite to tap on the barrels. It is polite to show your appreciation by
buying a bottle or two. Remember that vintners are extremely busy during
the harvest and the vendange.

You might want to ask the winemaker some of these questions:

> *What variety of grapes are grown?*
> *What is the yield per acre?*
> *How much wine is produced per year?*
> *Which are the best vintages?*
> *How are fermentation temperatures controlled?*
> *How are the wines aged? And for how long?*

The North American Vintner's Year

In the Vineyards

January   Vines are pruned.

February   Pruning continues, cuttings are placed in greenhouses.

March   Soil is aerated by plowing around the base of the vines, vines begin to come out of their winter sleep.

April   Cuttings are grafted onto rootstock to replace damaged vines. More plowing.

May   Flower buds open (and are threatened by late frosts). Vines are sprayed against mildew, suckers pruned.

June   Leaves and flower clusters develop, shoots and clusters are pruned, shoots tied to wires.

July   Grapes begin to develop, vines are sprayed against mildew and fungi, shoots are trimmed.

August   Grapes begin to ripen, sugar levels increase, acidity decreases, and bulk increases. Vineyards weeded and vines trimmed.

September   Acids continue to decrease, sugar continues to increase. Grapes are ready when sugar levels stop rising (approximately 40-45 days altogether). Grapes are harvested, vendange begins.

October   Vendange continues. Excess vegetation and fertilizer spread on the vines, noble rot (a benevolent fungus) reduces water content of grapes left on the vine for the production of ice wine.

November   Bases of vines are covered for protection, soil aerated.

December   Shoots are trimmed.

In the Cellar

January   Wine stocks from previous vintages, now in barrels, are maintained. Barrels are topped up, their bungs sterilized periodically with sulfur dioxide. Labelling and packing boxes of bottled wine for shipment is often done.

February   New wine from previous vintage is "racked off" into clean barrels to help it clear. The wine is often "assembled" in one or two large vats first, to eliminate variations between individual barrels, before being re-barreled.

March   Racking must finish before month end, some secondary fermentation occurs around the beginning of spring. Barrels must be continuously topped off, no "ullage" (empty space) allowed in casks.

April   Topping-off is still performed. About five percent of wine aged in traditional wooden barrels is lost to evaporation each year it spends in the wood.

May   Just before the vines flower, a second racking off of previous vintage is done to take the wine off its lees (sediment).

June   Racking continues, finishing the new wine and racking off all wines in barrel storage in the cellar. Warm weather makes cask maintenance a doubly important chore.

July   All efforts are devoted to maintaining a cool constant cellar temperature. Some bottling is done.

August   Inspections are conducted, as well as cleaning and maintenance of vats, tanks and barrels to be used in the up-coming vintage.

September All working metal parts of tanks and presses are treated with anti-rust varnish. The main cuverie or fermenting tank is thoroughly scoured, any wooden vessels used in fermentation are filled with water to swell the wood.

October While the vintage continues and new wine is beginning fermentation, year-old wine gets a final racking and the barrels are moved to "second year" cellaring for storage.

November Racking and "fining" or filtering of wine ready to be bottled. Bottling is the big job. Lusty new wine is often ready to be racked first, toward the end of the month.

December Constant topping up of casks begins. Bottling, labelling and packaging of older wine continues.

Tasting & Scoring Wines

How to Taste Wines

Pour an ounce or two of wine into a clean, clear glass. Look at the color of the wine against a light. Take note of the shade and density. Swirl the wine around the glass. Look at how the liquid coats the glass and how slowly it falls. Inhale the bouquet and try to differentiate between the aromas.

Roll a small sample around on your tongue. Breathe in over the wine on your tongue and try to differentiate between the tastes. Swallow and take note of the taste and aftertaste. Make some notes.

The aroma wheel on the following page will help you to pinpoint the wine's aromas. First, choose an adjective in the wheel's smallest circle, which contains the most general terms. Then move to the second circle and finally to the third (outer) circle, which contain more and more specific aroma descriptions. By defining a specific aroma, you will better remember the wine when you next taste it.

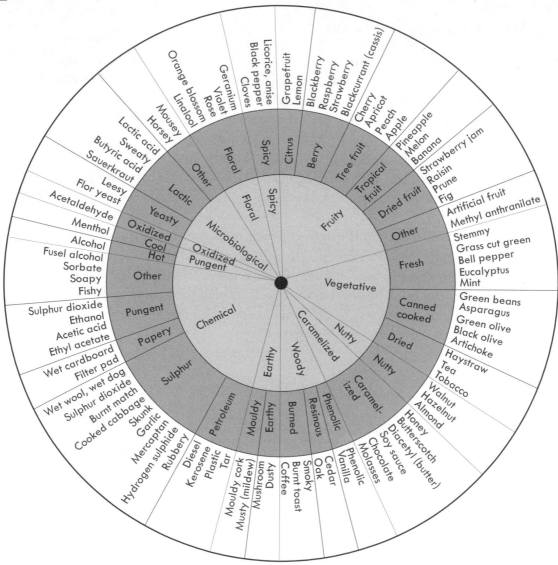

devised at the University of California at Davis by Ann C. Noble, et al.

How to Score Wines

Refer to the journal section "Tasting Notes" to record the wines you have sampled, and your impressions. The basic qualities to comment on are:

Date Tasted:
Name of Wine:
Occasion:
Food Eaten With Wine:
Other Guests:
Producer/Vintner:
Vintage:
Region: *some labels tell you the region or village of the winery*
Grape(s): *the variety of grape(s) is often noted on the label*
Price:
Appearance: *here you can note color, clarity, viscosity, depth of color, etc.*
Bouquet: *the smell of the wine, often complex and referring to more than aroma*
Taste: *here you can note sweetness, tannin, acidity, and finish*
Body & Balance: *body refers to the weight or fullness of a wine, and balance refers to a wine's alcoholic strength, acidity, residual sugar and tannins*
Comments:

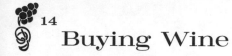

Buying Wine

Reading Wine Labels

The Rest of the World

Wine labels from North and South America, Australia and South Africa are almost always easy to understand. Wines from these countries are labeled and marketed by grape variety, which appears on the label second only in prominence to the name of the winery. The vintage year and/or geographical area may be specified in smaller type under the grape variety. For example, a California Chardonnay label will read:

ROBERT MONDAVI
CHARDONNAY
Napa Valley
(vintage)

Most "New World" wine labels follow this pattern with slight variation. European countries, however, have wine regulation and naming systems which have evolved over centuries and give prominence to geographical area rather than grape variety. In recent years, European wine producers have begun redesigning labels to more prominently display the grape variety, in response to international market pressure. For example, a generic red Burgundy which used to be labelled "Vin de Bourgogne" will now prominently proclaim itself "Pinot Noir."

France

The Appellation Contrôlée (AC) is France's primary system of regulating wine. It grants producers the right to use a "controlled name" as a guarantee of geographical origin, grape varieties used and quantity of wine produced from a specific acreage. Approximately one third of all French wines qualify

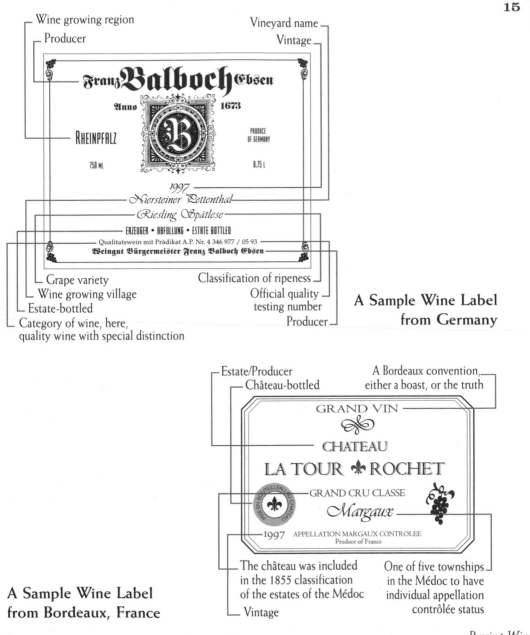

Wine growing region
Producer
Vineyard name
Vintage

Franz Balboch Ebsen

Anno 1673

RHEINPFALZ

PRODUCE OF GERMANY

750 ML   0.75 L

1997
Niersteiner Pettenthal
Riesling Spätlese
ERZEUGER • ABFULLUNG • ESTATE BOTTLED
Qualitatswein mit Prädikat A.P. Nr. 4 346 977 / 05 93
Weingut Bürgermeister Franz Balboch Ebsen

Grape variety
Wine growing village
Estate-bottled
Category of wine, here,
quality wine with special distinction

Classification of ripeness
Official quality
testing number
Producer

**A Sample Wine Label
from Germany**

Estate/Producer
Château-bottled

A Bordeaux convention,
either a boast, or the truth

GRAND VIN

CHATEAU

LA TOUR ✦ ROCHET

GRAND CRU CLASSE

Margaux

1997   APPELLATION MARGAUX CONTROLEE
Produce of France

The château was included
in the 1855 classification
of the estates of the Médoc

Vintage

One of five townships
in the Médoc to have
individual appellation
contrôlée status

**A Sample Wine Label
from Bordeaux, France**

for the AC. Wines that do not qualify may be labelled VDQS (Vins Delimites de Qualite Superieure) or Vins de Pays. These latter categories are where real bargains and unique specialty wines can often be found.

Italy
The Denominazione di Origine Controllata (DOC) was introduced only in the mid-20th century as the Italian answer to the French AC. The best guide to quality in Italian wines is usually the name of the producer.

Germany
German wine labels are actually the simplest to read. Dry wines and simple wines for everyday drinking are labelled Tafelwein (table wine). The labeling of quality wines made from Riesling grapes is based on the amount of sugar contained in the grapes at harvest. Wines made from grapes possessing the requisite natural sugars qualify for the designation Qualitätswein mit Prädikat (QmP). Within the QmP, wines are further designated by the following terms (in *ascending* order of concentration, sweetness, rarity, and price): Kabinett, Spätlese, Auslese, Beerenauslese, Trockenbeerenauslese, and finally Icewein, which is usually found only in very expensive half-bottles.

Spain
Tempranillo is the primary red grape, with local varieties sometimes identified. Labels indicate the geographical area of origin. The province of Rioja is justly famed for its massive reds, but other areas, such as Castilla y Leon, Valdepenas and Catalonia, now produce excellent red and white wines as modern methods are introduced.

A General Note

The term "Reserva" on Spanish reds indicates, as do variant spellings in Italy and in South America, wines that have been set aside for extra aging in oak. Reserva/riserva wines may carry very similar labels to the basic "house" version of the wine, and even come from the same vintage, but are slightly more expensive, reflecting their greater complexity and aging potential achieved through being held back in a barrel for a longer period.

Grape Varieties

White Varieties

Chardonnay — From Burgundy, used in Champagne. Wine is gold and bouquet broadens with aging, and grows drier with age.

Chenin Blanc — From the Loire. Pale greenish in color, light bodied and acidic, used extensively in South Africa and California.

Gewürztraminer — From Alsace. Pale straw in color, light bodied and spicily crisp although it can be quite sweet.

Müller-Thurgau — Most common German grape. A light and fresh cross between Riesling and Sylvaner.

Muscat — From France and Italy. Can create dry light wines or sweet full-bodied wines.

Pinot Gris — From Alsace originally but common in Northern Italy. Pale straw in color, produces light fruity wines.

Riesling — From Germany but also common in South Africa. Fresh, light and pale green when young but ripens to full, round, sweet and deep gold in color when aged.

Sauvignon Blanc	From the Loire and Bordeaux. Light, fresh and fruity when young, grows soft and subtle.
Sémillon	From Bordeaux, the source of the dessert wines of Sauternes and Barsac. Now widely used in Australia. Often combined with Chardonnay, to make dry table wines of great depth and style.
Trebbiano	Italian. Sharp and acidic. Used in blending, in the Cognac region it is used for distilling.
Viognier	Once a rare white Rhone wine, it is now making a comeback in France and appearing in California as an alternative wine to Chardonnay.

Red Varieties

Cabernet Sauvignon	The great grape of Bordeaux. Dark red and full-bodied, it takes years to reach optimum maturity.
Gamay	The grape of Beaujolais. A light and lively attractive wine which does not usually require aging.
Merlot	Used in Bordeaux, Pomerol and St. Emilion. Ruby red and tannic.
Nebbiolo	From Piedmont in Italy, smooth and fruity, can be powerful and tannic in Barolo and Barbaresco. Ages wonderfully.
Pinot Noir	The red grape of Burgundy and also Champagne. Full bodied flavor which is achieved with less maturing than Cabernet.

Pinotage	A hybrid red grape developed in South Africa. A cross between Pinot Noir and Cinsault, to withstand the heat while retaining the character of Pinot Noir.
Sangiovese	The most widely used red grape variety in Italy, where it is used to make the fine wines of Chianti, as well as carafe wines.
Syrah (Shiraz)	Used in Côte du Rhone, Australia and South Africa to produce dark, heavy and dry wines.
Tempranillo	Used in Spanish Rioja. Dark red, full-bodied and does well with aging.
Zinfandel	This Californian grape can produce light fresh wines or rich full-bodied ones.

Vintners around the world, especially in the New World, are continuously experimenting with combinations of grape varieties. These blends, often of two lower-grade grapes, can produce very palatable wines that are far better than the sum of their parts. Be adventurous—try them!

Storing & Serving Wine

Storing Wine

Best Temperatures
13° C (55° F)

Best Methods for Laying Down
Choose a well-ventilated, dry room, free from light and vibration, in the coolest part of the house. All wines bottles should be stored lying on their side in order to keep the corks from drying out. Make sure you can reach whichever bottles you want without having to disturb the others. Keep white wines in the coolest section of the room, perhaps close to the floor. Specially built wine cellars are available. Use the "Cellar Records" section of this book to record purchases and locations.

The Parts of a Wine Bottle

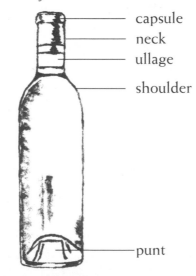

capsule

neck

ullage

shoulder

punt

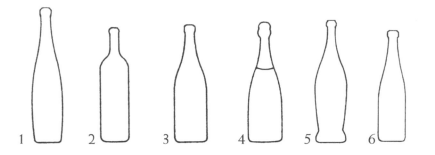

Some Common Bottle Shapes

1. **Alsace:** The *flute d'Alsace* is usually slightly taller than German bottles, with a punt and green glass.

2. **Bordeaux:** This is the classic shouldered bottle for red wines, with punt. Used worldwide. It may have to be stored laying on its side. These bottles come in a dark to pale green glass.

3. **Burgundy:** This is a slope-shouldered bottle, with a punt, used world-wide. The glass is medium to dark green for red and white wines.

4. **Champagne:** This bottle is slope-shouldered with a punt. Its glass is usually dark green and thicker than glass used for still wines so that it can withstand the pressure. These bottles are used for most sparkling wines. A magnum is the same shape, but twice the size.

5. **Côte de Provence:** This is the traditional bottle for all types of Provence wines.

6. **German Wine Bottle:** The bottles of Mosel wine are green, the others brown. The shape is similar to the *flute d'Alsace*.

A Sample Cellar

What is in your cellar will be dictated as much by budget and availability as by taste. Here is a sample collection which should give you enough variety to provide for any occasion. Ideally, you will replace each bottle consumed with two bottles, and slowly build up your cellar.

Begin with 48 bottles

2 red Bordeaux	2 red Burgundies	2 "Cru" Beaujolais
2 red Rhones	4 Italian reds	2 Spanish reds
2 Chilean reds	2 California reds	2 South African reds
2 Australian reds	2 Italian whites	2 California whites
2 Australian whites	2 Chilean whites	2 South African whites
2 white Burgundies	2 white Bordeaux	2 Alsatian whites
2 German Mosels	2 German Rhines	2 British Columbian whites
2 dessert wines	2 sparkling wines	

Serving Wine

Decanting

The English are great believers in decanting wine. The French almost never do it. Vintage ports, clarets and Burgundies that have developed a sediment on the bottom of the bottle can benefit from careful decanting. The same is also true of young, unripened wines, which benefit from the contact with the air. It enables them to undergo a rapid maturing process, whereby any harsh flavors become more rounded and softer. On the other hand, fine old wines would be ruined by decanting. They are best consumed within half an hour of opening.

Glass Shapes

Glasses should be clear and big enough that a serving fills only the bottom half of the glass. They should flare inwards to preserve the aroma of the wine.

1. **Champagne Flute**: Designed to prolong the wine's vivacity.

2. **Brandy Snifter**: Encourages warming of the brandy in the palm of the hand.

3. **Baden Römer**: For Rhine wine.

4. **Port or Dock-glass**

5. **Paris Goblet**: Suitable for red wines when several are served.

6. **I.N.A.O.** (*Institut National des Appellations d'Origine*): Specially designed for tasting all wines and spirits.

7. **Tulip**: An all-purpose glass suitable for red and white wines or for whites when several wines are served.

8. **Sherry Copita**

9. **Rhine and Mosel**

Opening and Serving

Invest in a good corkscrew which pushes down on the bottle at the same time as it draws the cork up and out. Open red wines an hour or so before serving. The host or hostess should pour a little wine into his or her own glass first to ensure that the guests do not get any crumbled cork that may have made its way into the bottle.

Fill each glass one-half full, then complete filling your own. A fresh glass for each new type of wine served is always a nice gesture but may not be practical, say, on a picnic in a kayak.

Champagne bottles should be opened by holding the bottle angled 45° away from you (to avoid damage to your eyes from flying corks). Hold the cork and turn the *bottle* until the cork comes away. Have a glass ready in case any precious drops of the champagne come frothing out.

Wine and Food

Wine and food are meant to go together and each complements the other. In general, the rule "white wine with fish and red wine with meat," is a good guideline but don't feel compelled to follow it slavishly. An overly hearty wine such as an unfiltered Côte du Rhone could overpower a subtle taste such as tuna carpaccio and a spicy chili would overwhelm a delicate Chardonnay.

If you are serving more than one wine with a meal, you might find these guidelines helpful:

white before red
young before old
dry before sweet
light before heavy

However, do not be intimidated by wine snobbery. The point is to enjoy yourself.

Some Truly Great Combinations:
port and Stilton
Muscadet and oysters
Burgundy and steak and mushrooms
Sauternes and pâté de foie gras
champagne and caviar

Hosting a Wine-Tasting Party

Most wine-tastings are wonderfully informal: a friend or two, an interesting but unfamiliar bottle of wine, glasses and a corkscrew.

You can host a more serious wine-tasting at home, which combines the best features of the critical and the convivial.

Sample a selection of no more than six similar wines, ideally from the same vintage, region and grape variety. Comparing Cabernet Sauvignon against Shiraz or Sangiovese is like comparing apples and oranges. Even if you spit out the wine, the discriminatory powers of tastebuds deteriorate markedly after six sips, so you might as well swallow and enjoy. If this is a co-operative event (and it should be), every guest or couple could be asked to bring a specific contribution for tasting. Make sure that your directions as to the wine you want are completely clear. Six people or twelve (six couples) is a good number, since each bottle divides into six full glasses or twelve "tasting-size" two-ounce samples.

Hold the tasting first—no drinking beforehand to blunt the tastebuds. You have the rest of the evening to relax and imbibe uncritically.

If you have twelve guests and want to provide a fresh glass for each of six wines, you'll need 72 glasses. Alternatively, you can issue everyone a single glass and provide facilities for rinsing it. This is the simplest way to go, as long as you have plenty of clean, lint-free linen napkins on hand to wipe down glasses and a carafe of neutral distilled water to rinse the glasses and the mouths of tasters between tastings.

If you are lucky enough to have access to six decanters, decant the six chosen wines half an hour before showtime, provided they are not the type that will expire before being tasted. If you choose not to decant, a sheet of paper carefully taped around the bottle to hide the label will suffice. Just be careful to pick the bottle up by the shoulder and bottom while pouring, or it may slide out of the improvised sleeve with disastrous results. Number each sleeve with a felt pen so no one gets confused about which wine they're drinking.

Provide tasting notes, photocopied from the journal (pages 57-127), for each guest and keep the journal to record this event for posterity.

Serve everyone the same wine at the same time, so you're all talking about the same subject, before moving to the next.

As for food, serve nothing but light French bread, small slices of baguette, and water to clear the palate during the tasting phase. Save the feast for after.

In the wine trade, this is referred to as a horizontal tasting. It is more informative to wine buyers as it provides a chance to assess a wine in the company of its direct competitors. At the end of the tasting, you may want to disclose the prices of each of the wines tasted and discuss which wines represent the best value.

After trying a number of horizontal tastings, you may want to experiment with a vertical tasting. This is a tasting of different vintages of the same wine. As vintage wine can be expensive, it's a good idea to ask each person (or couple) participating to provide a bottle. A vertical tasting allows you and your friends to compare notes on how a wine from a single house varies and changes with time. Whatever style of wine-tasting you try, above all, enjoy!

GRAND VIN

Wineries
Visited

MISE EN BOUTEILLE AU CHATEAU

APPELLATION
CONTROLEE

GRAND CRU CLASSE

e 75 cl. 10.5% vol.

30

Date
_____

Name of Winery   Location
_____

Grapes Grown
_____

Wines Produced
_____

Vintages Tasted
_____

Comments on Tastings
_____

_____

Vintages Purchased
_____

Date
_____

Name of Winery   Location
_____

Grapes Grown
_____

Wines Produced
_____

Vintages Tasted
_____

Comments on Tastings
_____

_____

Vintages Purchased
_____

Wineries Visited

Date

Name of Winery   Location

Grapes Grown

Wines Produced

Vintages Tasted

Comments on Tastings

Vintages Purchased

Date

Name of Winery   Location

Grapes Grown

Wines Produced

Vintages Tasted

Comments on Tastings

Vintages Purchased

Wineries Visited

Date

Name of Winery   Location

Grapes Grown

Wines Produced

Vintages Tasted

Comments on Tastings

Vintages Purchased

Date

Name of Winery   Location

Grapes Grown

Wines Produced

Vintages Tasted

Comments on Tastings

Vintages Purchased

Date

Name of Winery   Location

Grapes Grown

Wines Produced

Vintages Tasted

Comments on Tastings

Vintages Purchased

Date

Name of Winery   Location

Grapes Grown

Wines Produced

Vintages Tasted

Comments on Tastings

Vintages Purchased

Date

Name of Winery   Location

Grapes Grown

Wines Produced

Vintages Tasted

Comments on Tastings

Vintages Purchased

Date

Name of Winery   Location

Grapes Grown

Wines Produced

Vintages Tasted

Comments on Tastings

Vintages Purchased

GRAND VIN

Cellar
Records

APPELLATION
CONTROLEE

GRAND CRU CLASSE

e75 cl. 10.5% vol.

Wine   Vintage

Region   Producer/Shipper

Grape Variety

Place of Purchase   Date Purchased   Product Code

Price   Cellar Location

Optimum Date for Consumption

Comments

GRAND VIN

CHATEAU

de VOTRE ✤ MAISON

GRAND CRU CLASSE

Margaux

MISE EN BOUTEILLEAU AU CHATEAU

1998   APPELLATION MARGAUX CONTROLEE

paste your wine label here

Wine   Vintage

Region   Producer/Shipper

Grape Variety

Place of Purchase   Date Purchased   Product Code

Price   Cellar Location

Optimum Date for Consumption

Comments

GRAND VIN

CHATEAU

de VOTRE ⚜ MAISON

GRAND CRU CLASSE

Margaux

APPELLATION MARGAUX CONTROLEE

1998

MISE EN BOUTEILLEAU AU CHATEAU

paste your wine label here

Wine _____ Vintage _____

Region _____ Producer/Shipper _____

Grape Variety _____

Place of Purchase _____ Date Purchased _____ Product Code

Price _____ Cellar Location _____

Optimum Date for Consumption _____

Comments _____

paste your wine label here

Wine _____ Vintage _____

Region _____ Producer/Shipper _____

Grape Variety _____

Place of Purchase _____ Date Purchased _____ Product Code

Price _____ Cellar Location _____

Optimum Date for Consumption _____

Comments _____

GRAND VIN

CHATEAU

de VOTRE ❧ MAISON

MISE EN BOUTEILLEAU AU CHATEAU

GRAND CRU CLASSE

Margaux

1998　APPELLATION MARGAUX CONTROLEE

paste your wine label here

Wine _____ Vintage _____

Region _____ Producer/Shipper _____

Grape Variety _____

Place of Purchase _____ Date Purchased _____ Product Code _____

Price _____ Cellar Location _____

Optimum Date for Consumption _____

Comments _____

GRAND VIN

CHATEAU

de VOTRE ✤ MAISON

GRAND CRU CLASSE

Margaux

MISE EN BOUTEILLEAU AU CHATEAU

1998   APPELLATION MARGAUX CONTROLEE

paste your wine label here

Wine

Vintage

Region

Producer/Shipper

Grape Variety

Place of Purchase

Date Purchased

Product Code

Price

Cellar Location

Optimum Date for Consumption

Comments

GRAND VIN

CHATEAU

de VOTRE ✠ MAISON

GRAND CRU CLASSE

Margaux

MISE EN BOUTEILLEAU AU CHATEAU

1998

APPELLATION MARGAUX CONTROLEE

paste your wine label here

Wine _____ Vintage _____

Region _____ Producer/Shipper _____

Grape Variety _____

Place of Purchase _____ Date Purchased _____ Product Code _____

Price _____ Cellar Location _____

Optimum Date for Consumption _____

Comments _____

GRAND VIN

CHATEAU

de VOTRE ✦ MAISON

GRAND CRU CLASSE

Margaux

1998   APPELLATION MARGAUX CONTROLEE

MISE EN BOUTEILLEAU AU CHATEAU

paste your wine label here

Wine   Vintage

Region   Producer/Shipper

Grape Variety

Place of Purchase   Date Purchased   Product Code

Price   Cellar Location

Optimum Date for Consumption

Comments

GRAND VIN

CHATEAU

de VOTRE ✤ MAISON

GRAND CRU CLASSE

Margaux

1998 APPELLATION MARGAUX CONTROLEE

MISE EN BOUTEILLEAU AU CHATEAU

paste your wine label here

Wine

Vintage

Region

Producer/Shipper

Grape Variety

Place of Purchase

Date Purchased

Product Code

Price

Cellar Location

Optimum Date for Consumption

Comments

GRAND VIN

CHATEAU
de VOTRE ✤ MAISON

GRAND CRU CLASSE

Margaux

1998   APPELLATION MARGAUX CONTROLEE

MISE EN BOUTEILLEAU AU CHATEAU

paste your wine label here

Wine _____   Vintage _____

Region _____   Producer/Shipper _____

Grape Variety _____

Place of Purchase _____   Date Purchased _____   Product Code _____

Price _____   Cellar Location _____

Optimum Date for Consumption _____

Comments _____

GRAND VIN

CHATEAU

de VOTRE ✚ MAISON

GRAND CRU CLASSE

Margaux

1998   APPELLATION MARGAUX CONTROLEE

MISE EN BOUTEILLE AU CHATEAU

paste your wine label here

Wine   Vintage

Region   Producer/Shipper

Grape Variety

Place of Purchase   Date Purchased   Product Code

Price   Cellar Location

Optimum Date for Consumption

Comments

GRAND VIN

CHATEAU

de VOTRE ✤ MAISON

GRAND CRU CLASSE

Margaux

1998   APPELLATION MARGAUX CONTROLEE

MSE EN BOUTEILLEAU AU CHATEAU

paste your wine label here

Wine _____ Vintage _____

Region _____ Producer/Shipper _____

Grape Variety _____

Place of Purchase _____ Date Purchased _____ Product Code

Price _____ Cellar Location _____

Optimum Date for Consumption _____

Comments _____

GRAND VIN

CHATEAU

de VOTRE ✤ MAISON

GRAND CRU CLASSE

Margaux

MISE EN BOUTEILLEAU AU CHATEAU

1998   APPELLATION MARGAUX CONTROLEE

paste your wine label here

Wine _____ Vintage _____

Region _____ Producer/Shipper _____

Grape Variety _____

Place of Purchase _____ Date Purchased _____ Product Code

Price _____ Cellar Location _____

Optimum Date for Consumption _____

Comments _____

GRAND VIN

CHATEAU

de VOTRE ✤ MAISON

GRAND CRU CLASSE

Margaux

APPELLATION MARGAUX CONTROLEE

MISE EN BOUTEILLEAU AU CHATEAU

1998

paste your wine label here

Wine

Vintage

Region

Producer/Shipper

Grape Variety

Place of Purchase

Date Purchased

Product Code

Price

Cellar Location

Optimum Date for Consumption

Comments

GRAND VIN

CHATEAU

de VOTRE ✣ MAISON

GRAND CRU CLASSE

Margaux

MISE EN BOUTEILLEAU AU CHATEAU

1998

APPELLATION MARGAUX CONTROLEE

paste your wine label here

Wine   Vintage

Region   Producer/Shipper

Grape Variety

Place of Purchase   Date Purchased   Product Code

Price   Cellar Location

Optimum Date for Consumption

Comments

GRAND VIN

CHATEAU

de VOTRE ✤ MAISON

GRAND CRU CLASSE

Margaux

MSE EN BOUTEILLEAU AU CHATEAU

1998   APPELLATION MARGAUX CONTROLEE

paste your wine label here

Wine _____ Vintage _____

Region _____ Producer/Shipper _____

Grape Variety _____

Place of Purchase _____ Date Purchased _____ Product Code

Price _____ Cellar Location _____

Optimum Date for Consumption _____

Comments _____

paste your wine label here

Wine   Vintage

Region   Producer/Shipper

Grape Variety

Place of Purchase   Date Purchased   Product Code

Price   Cellar Location

Optimum Date for Consumption

Comments

paste your wine label here

Cellar Records

Wine   Vintage

Region   Producer/Shipper

Grape Variety

Place of Purchase   Date Purchased   Product Code

Price   Cellar Location

Optimum Date for Consumption

Comments

GRAND VIN

CHATEAU

de VOTRE ✤ MAISON

GRAND CRU CLASSE

Margaux

MISE EN BOUTEILLEAU AU CHATEAU

1998

APPELLATION MARGAUX CONTROLEE

paste your wine label here

Cellar Records

Wine   Vintage

Region   Producer/Shipper

Grape Variety

Place of Purchase   Date Purchased   Product Code

Price   Cellar Location

Optimum Date for Consumption

Comments

paste your wine label here

Wine _____ Vintage _____

Region _____ Producer/Shipper _____

Grape Variety _____

Place of Purchase _____ Date Purchased _____ Product Code

Price _____ Cellar Location _____

Optimum Date for Consumption _____

Comments _____

GRAND VIN

CHATEAU

de VOTRE ⚜ MAISON

GRAND CRU CLASSE

Margaux

MISE EN BOUTEILLEAU AU CHATEAU

1998   APPELLATION MARGAUX CONTROLEE

paste your wine label here

Wine   Vintage

Region   Producer/Shipper

Grape Variety

Place of Purchase   Date Purchased   Product Code

Price   Cellar Location

Optimum Date for Consumption

Comments

GRAND VIN

CHATEAU

de VOTRE ✠ MAISON

GRAND CRU CLASSE

Margaux

APPELLATION MARGAUX CONTROLEE

MSE EN BOUTEILLEAU AU CHATEAU

1998

paste your wine label here

Cellar Records

Date Tasted _____ Wine _____

Occasion _____ Food Eaten With Wine _____

Other Guests _____

Producer/Vintner _____

Vintage _____ Region _____

Grape(s) _____ Price _____ Product Code _____

Appearance _____ Bouquet _____

Taste _____ Body & Balance _____

Comments _____

paste your wine label here

GRAND VIN

CHATEAU

de VOTRE ✦ MAISON

GRAND CRU CLASSE

Margaux

MISE EN BOUTEILLEAU AU CHATEAU

1998   APPELLATION MARGAUX CONTROLEE

Tasting Notes

Date Tasted _____ Wine _____

Occasion _____ Food Eaten With Wine _____

Other Guests _____

Producer/Vintner _____

Vintage _____ Region _____

Grape(s) _____ Price _____ Product Code _____

Appearance _____ Bouquet _____

Taste _____ Body & Balance _____

Comments _____

paste your wine label here

GRAND VIN

CHATEAU

de VOTRE ❖ MAISON

GRAND CRU CLASSE

Margaux

MISE EN BOUTEILLEAU AU CHATEAU

1998

APPELLATION MARGAUX CONTROLEE

Tasting Notes

Date Tasted _____ Wine _____

Occasion _____ Food Eaten With Wine _____

Other Guests _____

Producer/Vintner _____

Vintage _____ Region _____

Grape(s) _____ Price _____ Product Code

Appearance _____ Bouquet _____

Taste _____ Body & Balance _____

Comments _____

paste your wine label here

GRAND VIN

CHATEAU

de VOTRE ✠ MAISON

GRAND CRU CLASSE

Margaux

1998

APPELLATION MARGAUX CONTROLEE

MISE EN BOUTEILLEAU AU CHATEAU

Tasting Notes

Date Tasted

Wine

Occasion

Food Eaten With Wine

Other Guests

Producer/Vintner

Vintage

Region

Grape(s)

Price

Product Code

Appearance

Bouquet

Taste

Body & Balance

Comments

paste your wine label here

GRAND VIN

CHATEAU

de VOTRE ⚜ MAISON

GRAND CRU CLASSE

Margaux

APPELLATION MARGAUX CONTROLEE

1998

Tasting Notes

Date Tasted _____ Wine _____

Occasion _____ Food Eaten With Wine _____

Other Guests _____

Producer/Vintner _____

Vintage _____ Region _____

Grape(s) _____ Price _____ Product Code

Appearance _____ Bouquet _____

Taste _____ Body & Balance _____

Comments _____

paste your wine label here

GRAND VIN

CHATEAU

de VOTRE ✤ MAISON

GRAND CRU CLASSE

Margaux

1998

APPELLATION MARGAUX CONTROLEE

Tasting Notes

Date Tasted _____ Wine _____

Occasion _____ Food Eaten With Wine _____

Other Guests _____

Producer/Vintner _____

Vintage _____ Region _____

Grape(s) _____ Price _____ Product Code

Appearance _____ Bouquet _____

Taste _____ Body & Balance _____

Comments _____

paste your wine label here

GRAND VIN

CHATEAU

de VOTRE ✤ MAISON

GRAND CRU CLASSE

Margaux

1998   APPELLATION MARGAUX CONTROLEE

MISE EN BOUTEILLEAU AU CHATEAU

Tasting Notes

Date Tasted

Wine

Occasion

Food Eaten With Wine

Other Guests

Producer/Vintner

Vintage

Region

Grape(s)

Price

Product Code

Appearance

Bouquet

Taste

Body & Balance

Comments

paste your wine label here

GRAND VIN

CHATEAU

de VOTRE ✤ MAISON

GRAND CRU CLASSE

Margaux

APPELLATION MARGAUX CONTROLEE

MISE EN BOUTEILLEAU AU CHATEAU

1998

Tasting Notes

Date Tasted	Wine
Occasion	Food Eaten With Wine
Other Guests	
Producer/Vintner	
Vintage	Region
Grape(s)	Price Product Code
Appearance	Bouquet
Taste	Body & Balance
Comments	

paste your wine label here

GRAND VIN

CHATEAU

de VOTRE ✦ MAISON

GRAND CRU CLASSE

Margaux

1998   APPELLATION MARGAUX CONTROLEE

Tasting Notes

Date Tasted

Wine

Occasion

Food Eaten With Wine

Other Guests

Producer/Vintner

Vintage

Region

Grape(s)

Price

Product Code

Appearance

Bouquet

Taste

Body & Balance

Comments

paste your wine label here

GRAND VIN

CHATEAU

de VOTRE ✣ MAISON

GRAND CRU CLASSE

Margaux

1998   APPELLATION MARGAUX CONTROLEE

MISE EN BOUTEILLEAU AU CHATEAU

Tasting Notes

Date Tasted	Wine
Occasion	Food Eaten With Wine
Other Guests	
Producer/Vintner	
Vintage	Region
Grape(s)	Price Product Code
Appearance	Bouquet
Taste	Body & Balance
Comments	

paste your wine label here

GRAND VIN

CHATEAU

de VOTRE ✚ MAISON

GRAND CRU CLASSE

Margaux

MISE EN BOUTEILLE AU CHATEAU

1998

APPELLATION MARGAUX CONTROLEE

Tasting Notes

Date Tasted	Wine
Occasion	Food Eaten With Wine
Other Guests	
Producer/Vintner	
Vintage	Region
Grape(s)	Price Product Code
Appearance	Bouquet
Taste	Body & Balance
Comments	

paste your wine label here

GRAND VIN

CHATEAU

de VOTRE ✤ MAISON

GRAND CRU CLASSE

Margaux

1998   APPELLATION MARGAUX CONTROLEE

MISE EN BOUTEILLEAU AU CHATEAU

Tasting Notes

Date Tasted	Wine
Occasion	Food Eaten With Wine
Other Guests	
Producer/Vintner	
Vintage	Region
Grape(s)	Price Product Code
Appearance	Bouquet
Taste	Body & Balance
Comments	

paste your wine label here

GRAND VIN

CHATEAU

de VOTRE ✷ MAISON

GRAND CRU CLASSE

Margaux

1998   APPELLATION MARGAUX CONTROLEE

MISE EN BOUTEILLEAU AU CHATEAU

Tasting Notes

Date Tasted _____ Wine _____

Occasion _____ Food Eaten With Wine _____

Other Guests _____

Producer/Vintner _____

Vintage _____ Region _____

Grape(s) _____ Price _____ Product Code

Appearance _____ Bouquet _____

Taste _____ Body & Balance _____

Comments _____

paste your wine label here

GRAND VIN

CHATEAU

de VOTRE ✤ MAISON

GRAND CRU CLASSE

Margaux

1998   APPELLATION MARGAUX CONTROLEE

MISE EN BOUTEILLEAU AU CHATEAU

Tasting Notes

Date Tasted   Wine

Occasion   Food Eaten With Wine

Other Guests

Producer/Vintner

Vintage   Region

Grape(s)   Price   Product Code

Appearance   Bouquet

Taste   Body & Balance

Comments

paste your wine label here

GRAND VIN

CHATEAU

de VOTRE ❧ MAISON

GRAND CRU CLASSE

Margaux

1998   APPELLATION MARGAUX CONTROLEE

MISE EN BOUTEILLE AU CHATEAU

Tasting Notes

Date Tasted _____ Wine _____

Occasion _____ Food Eaten With Wine _____

Other Guests _____

Producer/Vintner _____

Vintage _____ Region _____

Grape(s) _____ Price _____ Product Code

Appearance _____ Bouquet _____

Taste _____ Body & Balance _____

Comments _____

_____

paste your wine label here

GRAND VIN

CHATEAU

de VOTRE ✤ MAISON

GRAND CRU CLASSE

Margaux

MISE EN BOUTEILLE AU CHATEAU

1998   APPELLATION MARGAUX CONTROLEE

Tasting Notes

Date Tasted

Wine

Occasion

Food Eaten With Wine

Other Guests

Producer/Vintner

Vintage

Region

Grape(s)

Price

Product Code

Appearance

Bouquet

Taste

Body & Balance

Comments

paste your wine label here

GRAND VIN

CHATEAU

de VOTRE ❖ MAISON

GRAND CRU CLASSE

Margaux

APPELLATION MARGAUX CONTROLEE

MISE EN BOUTEILLEAU AU CHATEAU

1998

Tasting Notes

Date Tasted _____ Wine _____

Occasion _____ Food Eaten With Wine _____

Other Guests _____

Producer/Vintner _____

Vintage _____ Region _____

Grape(s) _____ Price _____ Product Code

Appearance _____ Bouquet _____

Taste _____ Body & Balance _____

Comments _____

paste your wine label here

GRAND VIN

CHATEAU

de VOTRE ✣ MAISON

GRAND CRU CLASSE

Margaux

APPELLATION MARGAUX CONTROLEE

MISE EN BOUTEILLEAU AU CHATEAU

1998

Tasting Notes

Date Tasted _____ Wine _____

Occasion _____ Food Eaten With Wine _____

Other Guests _____

Producer/Vintner _____

Vintage _____ Region _____

Grape(s) _____ Price _____ Product Code

Appearance _____ Bouquet _____

Taste _____ Body & Balance _____

Comments _____

paste your wine label here

GRAND VIN

CHATEAU

de VOTRE ❧ MAISON

GRAND CRU CLASSE

Margaux

MIS EN BOUTEILLEAU AU CHATEAU

1998

APPELLATION MARGAUX CONTROLEE

Tasting Notes

Date Tasted   Wine

Occasion   Food Eaten With Wine

Other Guests

Producer/Vintner

Vintage   Region

Grape(s)   Price   Product Code

Appearance   Bouquet

Taste   Body & Balance

Comments

paste your wine label here

GRAND VIN

CHATEAU

de VOTRE ✤ MAISON

GRAND CRU CLASSE

Margaux

1998

APPELLATION MARGAUX CONTROLEE

MISE EN BOUTEILLEAU AU CHATEAU

Tasting Notes

Date Tasted	Wine

Occasion	Food Eaten With Wine

Other Guests

Producer/Vintner

Vintage	Region

Grape(s)	Price	Product Code

Appearance	Bouquet

Taste	Body & Balance

Comments

paste your wine label here

GRAND VIN

CHATEAU

de VOTRE ✤ MAISON

GRAND CRU CLASSE

Margaux

MISE EN BOUTEILLE AU CHATEAU

1998   APPELLATION MARGAUX CONTROLEE

Tasting Notes

Date Tasted	Wine
Occasion	Food Eaten With Wine
Other Guests	
Producer/Vintner	
Vintage	Region
Grape(s)	Price — Product Code
Appearance	Bouquet
Taste	Body & Balance
Comments	

paste your wine label here

GRAND VIN

CHATEAU

de VOTRE ✣ MAISON

GRAND CRU CLASSE

Margaux

MISE EN BOUTEILLEAU AU CHATEAU

1998 — APPELLATION MARGAUX CONTROLEE

Tasting Notes

Date Tasted   Wine

Occasion   Food Eaten With Wine

Other Guests

Producer/Vintner

Vintage   Region

Grape(s)   Price   Product Code

Appearance   Bouquet

Taste   Body & Balance

Comments

paste your wine label here

GRAND VIN

CHATEAU

de VOTRE ✦ MAISON

GRAND CRU CLASSE

Margaux

1998   APPELLATION MARGAUX CONTROLEE

MISE EN BOUTEILLEAU AU CHATEAU

Tasting Notes

Date Tasted	Wine

Occasion	Food Eaten With Wine

Other Guests

Producer/Vintner

Vintage	Region

Grape(s)	Price	Product Code

Appearance	Bouquet

Taste	Body & Balance

Comments

paste your wine label here

GRAND VIN

CHATEAU

de VOTRE ✣ MAISON

GRAND CRU CLASSE

Margaux

1998   APPELLATION MARGAUX CONTROLEE

MISE EN BOUTEILLEAU AU CHATEAU

Tasting Notes

Date Tasted	Wine
Occasion	Food Eaten With Wine
Other Guests	
Producer/Vintner	
Vintage	Region
Grape(s)	Price Product Code
Appearance	Bouquet
Taste	Body & Balance
Comments	

paste your wine label here

GRAND VIN

CHATEAU

de VOTRE ❧ MAISON

GRAND CRU CLASSE

Margaux

MISE EN BOUTEILLEAU AU CHATEAU

1998   APPELLATION MARGAUX CONTROLEE

Tasting Notes

Date Tasted | Wine

Occasion | Food Eaten With Wine

Other Guests

Producer/Vintner

Vintage | Region

Grape(s) | Price | Product Code

Appearance | Bouquet

Taste | Body & Balance

Comments

paste your wine label here

GRAND VIN

CHATEAU

de VOTRE ✤ MAISON

GRAND CRU CLASSE

Margaux

1998 APPELLATION MARGAUX CONTROLEE

MISE EN BOUTEILLEAU AU CHATEAU

Tasting Notes

Date Tasted   Wine

Occasion   Food Eaten With Wine

Other Guests

Producer/Vintner

Vintage   Region

Grape(s)   Price   Product Code

Appearance   Bouquet

Taste   Body & Balance

Comments

paste your wine label here

GRAND VIN

CHATEAU

de VOTRE ✤ MAISON

GRAND CRU CLASSE

Margaux

1998   APPELLATION MARGAUX CONTROLEE

Tasting Notes

Date Tasted _____ Wine _____

Occasion _____ Food Eaten With Wine _____

Other Guests _____

Producer/Vintner _____

Vintage _____ Region _____

Grape(s) _____ Price _____ Product Code

Appearance _____ Bouquet _____

Taste _____ Body & Balance _____

Comments _____

---

paste your wine label here

GRAND VIN

CHATEAU

de VOTRE ✤ MAISON

GRAND CRU CLASSE

Margaux

MISE EN BOUTEILLEAU AU CHATEAU

1998   APPELLATION MARGAUX CONTROLEE

Tasting Notes

Date Tasted   Wine

Occasion   Food Eaten With Wine

Other Guests

Producer/Vintner

Vintage   Region

Grape(s)   Price   Product Code

Appearance   Bouquet

Taste   Body & Balance

Comments

paste your wine label here

GRAND VIN

CHATEAU

de VOTRE ✤ MAISON

GRAND CRU CLASSE

Margaux

MISE EN BOUTEILLEAU AU CHATEAU

1998   APPELLATION MARGAUX CONTROLEE

Tasting Notes

Date Tasted

Wine

Occasion

Food Eaten With Wine

Other Guests

Producer/Vintner

Vintage

Region

Grape(s)

Price

Product Code

Appearance

Bouquet

Taste

Body & Balance

Comments

paste your wine label here

GRAND VIN

CHATEAU

de VOTRE ⚜ MAISON

GRAND CRU CLASSE

Margaux

1998   APPELLATION MARGAUX CONTROLEE

Tasting Notes

Date Tasted	Wine
Occasion	Food Eaten With Wine
Other Guests	
Producer/Vintner	
Vintage	Region
Grape(s)	Price Product Code
Appearance	Bouquet
Taste	Body & Balance
Comments	

paste your wine label here

GRAND VIN

CHATEAU

de VOTRE ❧ MAISON

GRAND CRU CLASSE

Margaux

1998   APPELLATION MARGAUX CONTROLEE

MISE EN BOUTEILLEAU AU CHATEAU

Tasting Notes

Date Tasted	Wine
Occasion	Food Eaten With Wine
Other Guests	
Producer/Vintner	
Vintage	Region
Grape(s)	Price Product Code
Appearance	Bouquet
Taste	Body & Balance
Comments	

paste your wine label here

GRAND VIN

CHATEAU

de VOTRE ✤ MAISON

GRAND CRU CLASSE

Margaux

1998   APPELLATION MARGAUX CONTROLEE

Tasting Notes

Date Tasted   Wine

Occasion   Food Eaten With Wine

Other Guests

Producer/Vintner

Vintage   Region

Grape(s)   Price   Product Code

Appearance   Bouquet

Taste   Body & Balance

Comments

paste your wine label here

GRAND VIN

CHATEAU

de VOTRE ✣ MAISON

GRAND CRU CLASSE

Margaux

1998   APPELLATION MARGAUX CONTROLEE

MISE EN BOUTEILLEAU AU CHATEAU

Tasting Notes

Date Tasted	Wine
Occasion	Food Eaten With Wine
Other Guests	
Producer/Vintner	
Vintage	Region
Grape(s)	Price Product Code
Appearance	Bouquet
Taste	Body & Balance
Comments	

paste your wine label here

GRAND VIN

CHATEAU

de VOTRE ✦ MAISON

GRAND CRU CLASSE

Margaux

1998   APPELLATION MARGAUX CONTROLEE

Tasting Notes

Date Tasted	Wine
Occasion	Food Eaten With Wine
Other Guests	
Producer/Vintner	
Vintage	Region
Grape(s)	Price ⸻ Product Code
Appearance	Bouquet
Taste	Body & Balance
Comments	

paste your wine label here

GRAND VIN

CHATEAU

de VOTRE ✤ MAISON

GRAND CRU CLASSE

Margaux

1998   APPELLATION MARGAUX CONTROLEE

MISE EN BOUTEILLEAU AU CHATEAU

Tasting Notes

Date Tasted   Wine

Occasion   Food Eaten With Wine

Other Guests

Producer/Vintner

Vintage   Region

Grape(s)   Price   Product Code

Appearance   Bouquet

Taste   Body & Balance

Comments

paste your wine label here

GRAND VIN

CHATEAU

de VOTRE ❧ MAISON

GRAND CRU CLASSE

Margaux

1998   APPELLATION MARGAUX CONTROLEE

MISE EN BOUTEILLEAU AU CHATEAU

Tasting Notes

Date Tasted _____ Wine _____

Occasion _____ Food Eaten With Wine _____

Other Guests _____

Producer/Vintner _____

Vintage _____ Region _____

Grape(s) _____ Price _____ Product Code

Appearance _____ Bouquet _____

Taste _____ Body & Balance _____

Comments _____

paste your wine label here

GRAND VIN

CHATEAU

de VOTRE ❧ MAISON

GRAND CRU CLASSE

Margaux

MISE EN BOUTEILLEAU AU CHATEAU

1998   APPELLATION MARGAUX CONTROLEE

Tasting Notes

Date Tasted   Wine

Occasion   Food Eaten With Wine

Other Guests

Producer/Vintner

Vintage   Region

Grape(s)   Price   Product Code

Appearance   Bouquet

Taste   Body & Balance

Comments

paste your wine label here

GRAND VIN

CHATEAU

de VOTRE ❖ MAISON

GRAND CRU CLASSE

Margaux

1998   APPELLATION MARGAUX CONTROLEE

MISE EN BOUTEILLEAU AU CHATEAU

Tasting Notes

Date Tasted _____ Wine _____

Occasion _____ Food Eaten With Wine _____

Other Guests _____

Producer/Vintner _____

Vintage _____ Region _____

Grape(s) _____ Price _____ Product Code _____

Appearance _____ Bouquet _____

Taste _____ Body & Balance _____

Comments _____

paste your wine label here

GRAND VIN

CHATEAU
de VOTRE ❧ MAISON

GRAND CRU CLASSE
Margaux

MISE EN BOUTEILLEAU AU CHATEAU

1998   APPELLATION MARGAUX CONTROLEE

Tasting Notes

Date Tasted _____ Wine _____

Occasion _____ Food Eaten With Wine _____

Other Guests _____

Producer/Vintner _____

Vintage _____ Region _____

Grape(s) _____ Price _____ Product Code _____

Appearance _____ Bouquet _____

Taste _____ Body & Balance _____

Comments _____

paste your wine label here

Tasting Notes

Date Tasted _____ Wine _____

Occasion _____ Food Eaten With Wine _____

Other Guests _____

Producer/Vintner _____

Vintage _____ Region _____

Grape(s) _____ Price _____ Product Code _____

Appearance _____ Bouquet _____

Taste _____ Body & Balance _____

Comments _____

paste your wine label here

GRAND VIN

CHATEAU

de VOTRE ✤ MAISON

GRAND CRU CLASSE

Margaux

MISE EN BOUTEILLEAU AU CHATEAU

1998 APPELLATION MARGAUX CONTROLEE

Tasting Notes

Date Tasted

Wine

Occasion

Food Eaten With Wine

Other Guests

Producer/Vintner

Vintage

Region

Grape(s)

Price

Product Code

Appearance

Bouquet

Taste

Body & Balance

Comments

paste your wine label here

Tasting Notes

Date Tasted _____ Wine _____

Occasion _____ Food Eaten With Wine _____

Other Guests _____

Producer/Vintner _____

Vintage _____ Region _____

Grape(s) _____ Price _____ Product Code _____

Appearance _____ Bouquet _____

Taste _____ Body & Balance _____

Comments _____

paste your wine label here

GRAND VIN

CHATEAU

de VOTRE ❧ MAISON

GRAND CRU CLASSE

Margaux

1998   APPELLATION MARGAUX CONTROLEE

MISE EN BOUTEILLEAU AU CHATEAU

Tasting Notes

Date Tasted   Wine

Occasion   Food Eaten With Wine

Other Guests

Producer/Vintner

Vintage   Region

Grape(s)   Price   Product Code

Appearance   Bouquet

Taste   Body & Balance

Comments

paste your wine label here

GRAND VIN

CHATEAU

de VOTRE ✣ MAISON

GRAND CRU CLASSE

Margaux

1998   APPELLATION MARGAUX CONTROLEE

MISE EN BOUTEILLEAU AU CHATEAU

Tasting Notes

Date Tasted _____ Wine _____

Occasion _____ Food Eaten With Wine _____

Other Guests _____

Producer/Vintner _____

Vintage _____ Region _____

Grape(s) _____ Price _____ Product Code

Appearance _____ Bouquet _____

Taste _____ Body & Balance _____

Comments _____

paste your wine label here

GRAND VIN

CHATEAU

de VOTRE ✤ MAISON

GRAND CRU CLASSE

Margaux

1998   APPELLATION MARGAUX CONTROLEE

Tasting Notes

Date Tasted _____ Wine _____

Occasion _____ Food Eaten With Wine _____

Other Guests _____

Producer/Vintner _____

Vintage _____ Region _____

Grape(s) _____ Price _____ Product Code

Appearance _____ Bouquet _____

Taste _____ Body & Balance _____

Comments _____

paste your wine label here

GRAND VIN

CHATEAU

de VOTRE ✤ MAISON

GRAND CRU CLASSE

Margaux

1998 APPELLATION MARGAUX CONTROLEE

MISE EN BOUTEILLEAU AU CHATEAU

Tasting Notes

Date Tasted	Wine

Occasion	Food Eaten With Wine

Other Guests

Producer/Vintner

Vintage	Region

Grape(s)	Price	Product Code

Appearance	Bouquet

Taste	Body & Balance

Comments

paste your wine label here

GRAND VIN

CHATEAU

de VOTRE ✣ MAISON

GRAND CRU CLASSE

Margaux

MISE EN BOUTEILLEAU AU CHATEAU

1998   APPELLATION MARGAUX CONTROLEE

Tasting Notes

Date Tasted	Wine	

Occasion	Food Eaten With Wine

Other Guests

Producer/Vintner

Vintage	Region

Grape(s)	Price	Product Code

Appearance	Bouquet

Taste	Body & Balance

Comments

paste your wine label here

GRAND VIN

CHATEAU

de VOTRE ✤ MAISON

GRAND CRU CLASSE

Margaux

1998   APPELLATION MARGAUX CONTROLEE

MISE EN BOUTEILLE AU CHATEAU

Tasting Notes

Date Tasted	Wine

Occasion	Food Eaten With Wine

Other Guests

Producer/Vintner

Vintage	Region

Grape(s)	Price	Product Code

Appearance	Bouquet

Taste	Body & Balance

Comments

paste your wine label here

GRAND VIN

CHATEAU

de VOTRE ✤ MAISON

GRAND CRU CLASSE

Margaux

1998 APPELLATION MARGAUX CONTROLEE

MISE EN BOUTEILLEAU AU CHATEAU

Tasting Notes

Date Tasted

Wine

Occasion

Food Eaten With Wine

Other Guests

Producer/Vintner

Vintage

Region

Grape(s)

Price

Product Code

Appearance

Bouquet

Taste

Body & Balance

Comments

paste your wine label here

GRAND VIN

CHATEAU

de VOTRE ✤ MAISON

GRAND CRU CLASSE

Margaux

1998

APPELLATION MARGAUX CONTROLEE

MISE EN BOUTEILLEAU AU CHATEAU

Tasting Notes

Date Tasted	Wine
Occasion	Food Eaten With Wine
Other Guests	
Producer/Vintner	
Vintage	Region
Grape(s)	Price Product Code
Appearance	Bouquet
Taste	Body & Balance
Comments	

paste your wine label here

GRAND VIN

CHATEAU

de VOTRE ✠ MAISON

GRAND CRU CLASSE

Margaux

1998 APPELLATION MARGAUX CONTROLEE

MISE EN BOUTEILLEAU AU CHATEAU

Tasting Notes

Date Tasted	Wine

Occasion	Food Eaten With Wine

Other Guests

Producer/Vintner

Vintage	Region

Grape(s)	Price	Product Code

Appearance	Bouquet

Taste	Body & Balance

Comments

paste your wine label here

GRAND VIN

CHATEAU

de VOTRE ✤ MAISON

GRAND CRU CLASSE

Margaux

1998 APPELLATION MARGAUX CONTROLEE

Tasting Notes

Date Tasted	Wine
Occasion	Food Eaten With Wine
Other Guests	
Producer/Vintner	
Vintage	Region
Grape(s)	Price Product Code
Appearance	Bouquet
Taste	Body & Balance
Comments	

paste your wine label here

GRAND VIN

CHATEAU

de VOTRE ✦ MAISON

GRAND CRU CLASSE

Margaux

1998   APPELLATION MARGAUX CONTROLEE

Tasting Notes

Date Tasted   Wine

Occasion   Food Eaten With Wine

Other Guests

Producer/Vintner

Vintage   Region

Grape(s)   Price   Product Code

Appearance   Bouquet

Taste   Body & Balance

Comments

paste your wine label here

GRAND VIN

CHATEAU

de VOTRE ❧ MAISON

GRAND CRU CLASSE

Margaux

1998   APPELLATION MARGAUX CONTROLEE

MISE EN BOUTEILLEAU AU CHATEAU

Tasting Notes

Date Tasted

Wine

Occasion

Food Eaten With Wine

Other Guests

Producer/Vintner

Vintage

Region

Grape(s)

Price

Product Code

Appearance

Bouquet

Taste

Body & Balance

Comments

paste your wine label here

GRAND VIN

CHATEAU

de VOTRE ❧ MAISON

GRAND CRU CLASSE

Margaux

1998   APPELLATION MARGAUX CONTROLEE

MISE EN BOUTEILLEAU AU CHATEAU

Tasting Notes

Date Tasted

Wine

Occasion

Food Eaten With Wine

Other Guests

Producer/Vintner

Vintage

Region

Grape(s)

Price

Product Code

Appearance

Bouquet

Taste

Body & Balance

Comments

paste your wine label here

GRAND VIN

CHATEAU

de VOTRE ✤ MAISON

GRAND CRU CLASSE

Margaux

1998 APPELLATION MARGAUX CONTROLEE

MSE EN BOUTEILLEAU AU CHATEAU

Tasting Notes

Date Tasted _____ Wine _____

Occasion _____ Food Eaten With Wine _____

Other Guests _____

Producer/Vintner _____

Vintage _____ Region _____

Grape(s) _____ Price _____ Product Code

Appearance _____ Bouquet _____

Taste _____ Body & Balance _____

Comments _____

paste your wine label here

GRAND VIN

CHATEAU

de VOTRE ✤ MAISON

GRAND CRU CLASSE

Margaux

1998   APPELLATION MARGAUX CONTROLEE

MISE EN BOUTEILLEAU AU CHATEAU

Tasting Notes

Date Tasted _____ Wine _____

Occasion _____ Food Eaten With Wine _____

Other Guests _____

Producer/Vintner _____

Vintage _____ Region _____

Grape(s) _____ Price _____ Product Code

Appearance _____ Bouquet _____

Taste _____ Body & Balance _____

Comments _____

paste your wine label here

GRAND VIN

CHATEAU

de VOTRE ✥ MAISON

GRAND CRU CLASSE

Margaux

APPELLATION MARGAUX CONTROLEE

MISE EN BOUTEILLEAU AU CHATEAU

1998

Tasting Notes

Date Tasted	Wine
Occasion	Food Eaten With Wine
Other Guests	
Producer/Vintner	
Vintage	Region
Grape(s)	Price Product Code
Appearance	Bouquet
Taste	Body & Balance
Comments	

paste your wine label here

GRAND VIN

CHATEAU

de VOTRE ✣ MAISON

GRAND CRU CLASSE

Margaux

MISE EN BOUTEILLEAU AU CHATEAU

1998   APPELLATION MARGAUX CONTROLEE

Tasting Notes

Date Tasted | Wine

Occasion | Food Eaten With Wine

Other Guests

Producer/Vintner

Vintage | Region

Grape(s) | Price | Product Code

Appearance | Bouquet

Taste | Body & Balance

Comments

paste your wine label here

GRAND VIN
CHATEAU
de VOTRE MAISON
MISE EN BOUTEILLEAU AU CHATEAU
GRAND CRU CLASSE
Margaux
1998
APPELLATION MARGAUX CONTROLEE

Date Tasted	Wine	
Occasion	Food Eaten With Wine	
Other Guests		
Producer/Vintner		
Vintage	Region	
Grape(s)	Price	Product Code
Appearance	Bouquet	
Taste	Body & Balance	
Comments		

paste your wine label here

GRAND VIN

CHATEAU

de VOTRE ✣ MAISON

GRAND CRU CLASSE

Margaux

MISE EN BOUTEILLE AU CHATEAU

1998 APPELLATION MARGAUX CONTROLEE

Tasting Notes

Date Tasted   Wine

Occasion   Food Eaten With Wine

Other Guests

Producer/Vintner

Vintage   Region

Grape(s)   Price   Product Code

Appearance   Bouquet

Taste   Body & Balance

Comments

paste your wine label here

Tasting Notes

Date Tasted	Wine
Occasion	Food Eaten With Wine
Other Guests	
Producer/Vintner	
Vintage	Region
Grape(s)	Price Product Code
Appearance	Bouquet
Taste	Body & Balance
Comments	

paste your wine label here

GRAND VIN

CHATEAU

de VOTRE ✤ MAISON

GRAND CRU CLASSE

Margaux

1998   APPELLATION MARGAUX CONTROLEE

MISE EN BOUTEILLEAU AU CHATEAU

Tasting Notes

Date Tasted _____ Wine _____

Occasion _____ Food Eaten With Wine _____

Other Guests _____

Producer/Vintner _____

Vintage _____ Region _____

Grape(s) _____ Price _____ Product Code

Appearance _____ Bouquet _____

Taste _____ Body & Balance _____

Comments _____

paste your wine label here

GRAND VIN

CHATEAU

de VOTRE ⚜ MAISON

GRAND CRU CLASSE

Margaux

1998   APPELLATION MARGAUX CONTROLEE

MISE EN BOUTEILLEAU AU CHATEAU

Tasting Notes

Date Tasted   Wine

Occasion   Food Eaten With Wine

Other Guests

Producer/Vintner

Vintage   Region

Grape(s)   Price   Product Code

Appearance   Bouquet

Taste   Body & Balance

Comments

paste your wine label here

Tasting Notes

Date Tasted	Wine
Occasion	Food Eaten With Wine
Other Guests	
Producer/Vintner	
Vintage	Region
Grape(s)	Price Product Code
Appearance	Bouquet
Taste	Body & Balance
Comments	

paste your wine label here

GRAND VIN

CHATEAU

de VOTRE ✤ MAISON

GRAND CRU CLASSE

Margaux

1998   APPELLATION MARGAUX CONTROLEE

Tasting Notes

Notes

Notes

Glossary of Terms

bouquet: the tasting term for the smell of wine, complex and often referring to more than the simple aroma of the grape

bung: a stopper for closing a hole, in wineries, the stopper used in barrels of aging wine

cuverie: the vat hall, where fermentation takes place

cru: growth (as in Premier cru, first growth, etc.)

fining: clarifying the wine by use of various substances such as egg whites, gelatin or bentonite

lees: sediment, such as dead yeast cells and grape skin particles, that settles at the bottom of a cask, barrel, etc.

noble rot: a benevolent fungus that attacks ripe, undamaged white wine grapes and can result in extremely sweet grapes. Used in long-living sweet wines.

racking: siphoning or pumping wines off the lees

tannins: a group of chemicals that give grapes astringency or bitterness. They are sensed in the mouth rather than the nose.

ullage: the amount by which a cask, bottle, etc., falls short of being full

vendange: the French word for harvest